42844830R00057

Made in the USA
Lexington, KY
20 June 2019